My Fair Lady

10 SELECTIONS FROM THE MUSICAL
Arranged by Dan Coates

My Fair Lady debuted on Broadway in 1956 and had an initial run of 2,717 performances—a record at the time. The original production starred Rex Harrison (Henry Higgins) and Julie Andrews (Eliza Doolittle). Based on the play *Pygmalion* by George Bernard Shaw, it tells the story of the "makeover" of Eliza Doolittle, a poor girl with a thick Cockney accent. Henry Higgins, a professor of phonetics, makes a bet with Colonel Pickering, a fellow linguist, that he can improve Eliza's speech, manners and appearance, all to pass her off as a true debutante. Eliza believes that these newfound skills will change her life completely ("Wouldn't It Be Loverly"). After intense and often times frustrating studies, everything comes together and she "fixes" her speech ("The Rain in Spain"). Eliza attends an Embassy Ball and convinces everyone, even a Hungarian phonetics expert, that she is a debutante. The musical ends with the possibility of romance between Henry and Eliza ("I've Grown Accustomed to Her Face").

My Fair Lady is still a beloved part of American musical theater today. With 3 revivals, 7 Tony Awards and 8 Academy® Awards to its credit, *My Fair Lady* truly is **Broadway's Best**!

Contents

Cover photo courtesy the Library of Congress

EXCLUSIVELY DISTRIBUTED BY

Copyright © MMVII by Alfred Publishing Co., Inc.
All rights reserved.   Printed in USA.
ISBN-13: 978-0-7390-4275-5

Wouldn't It Be Loverly

Lyrics by Alan Jay Lerner
Music by Frederick Loewe
Arranged by Dan Coates

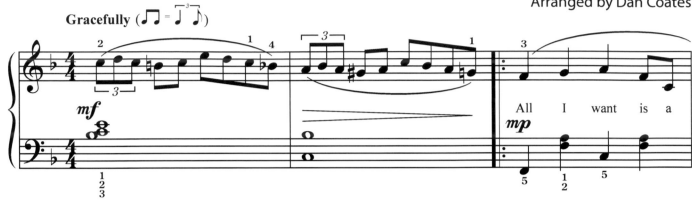

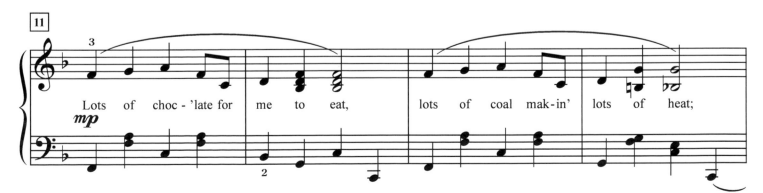

warm face, warm hands, warm feet, oh, would—n't it be

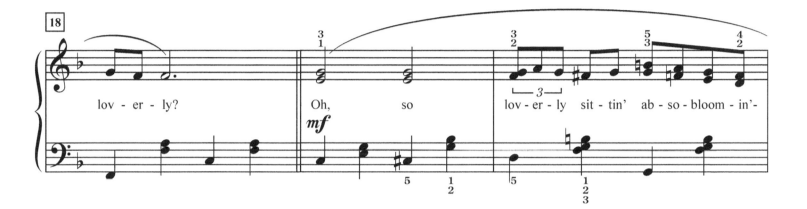

lov-er-ly? Oh, so lov-er-ly sit-tin' ab-so-bloom-in'-

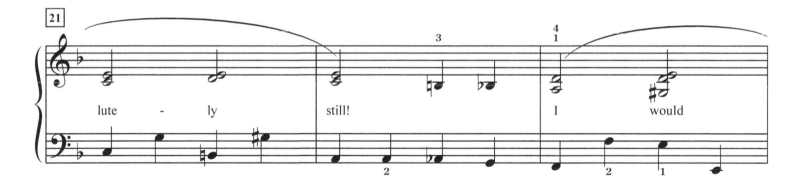

lute—ly still! I would

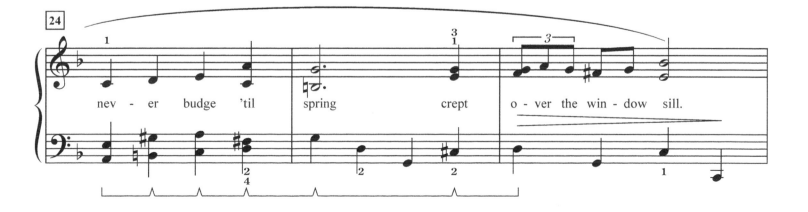

nev—er budge 'til spring crept o-ver the win-dow sill.

Some-one's head rest-in' on my knee, warm and ten - der as he can be;

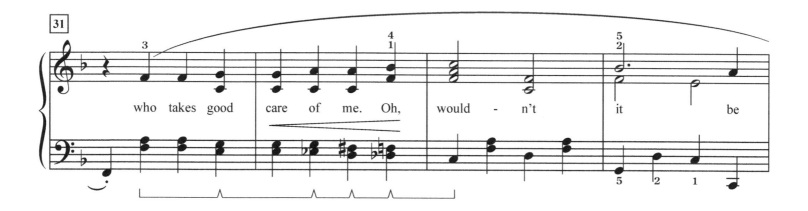

who takes good care of me. Oh, would - n't it be

1. lov - er - ly?   2. lov - er - ly?   Lov - er - ly!

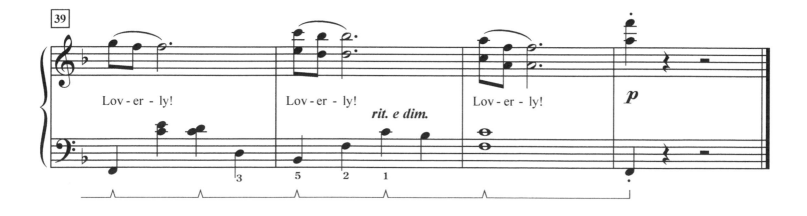

Lov - er - ly!   Lov - er - ly!   Lov - er - ly!

With a Little Bit of Luck

Lyrics by Alan Jay Lerner
Music by Frederick Loewe
Arranged by Dan Coates

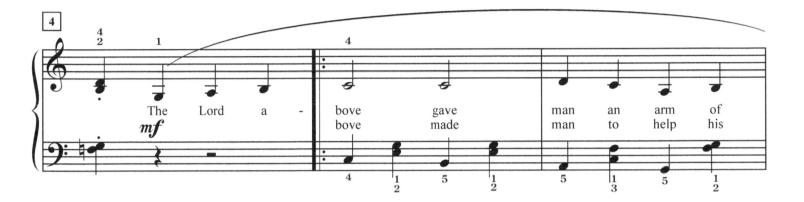

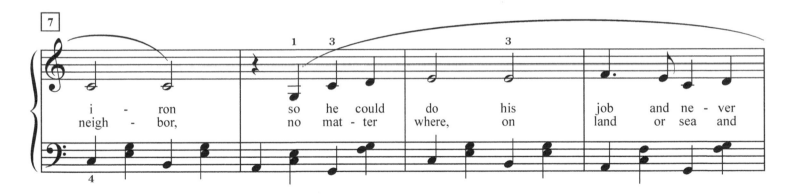

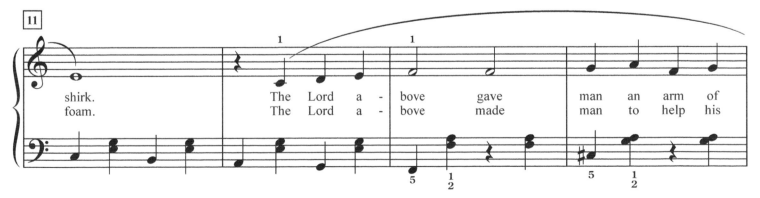

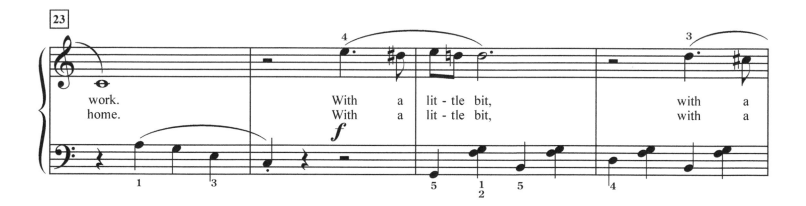

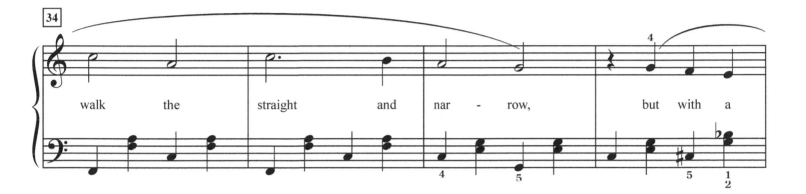

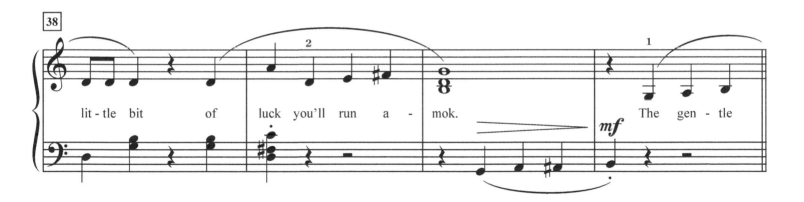

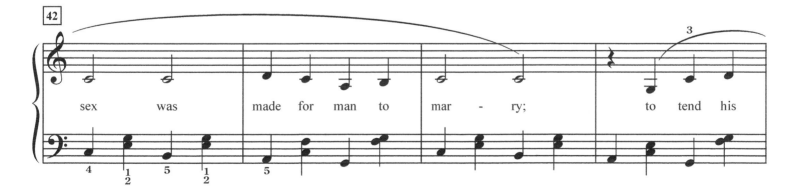

needs and see his food is cooked. The gen - tle

sex was made for man to mar - ry, but with a

lit - tle bit of luck, with a lit - tle bit of luck, you can

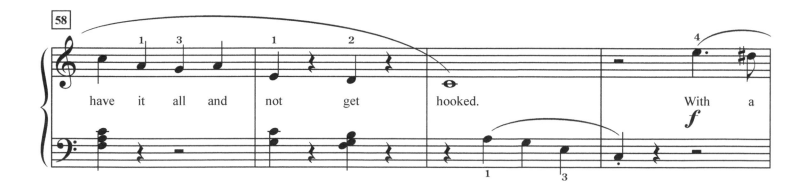

have it all and not get hooked. With a

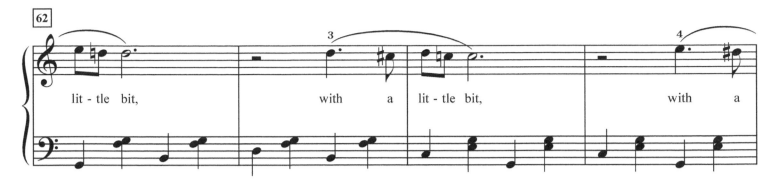

lit - tle bit, with a lit - tle bit, with a

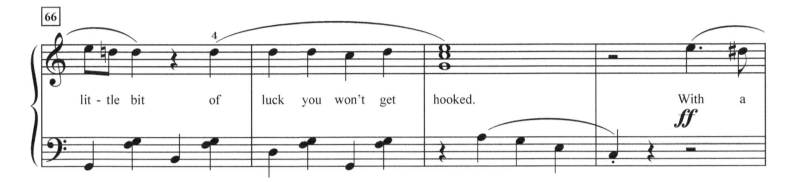

lit - tle bit of luck you won't get hooked. With a
ff

lit - tle bit, with a lit - tle bit, with a

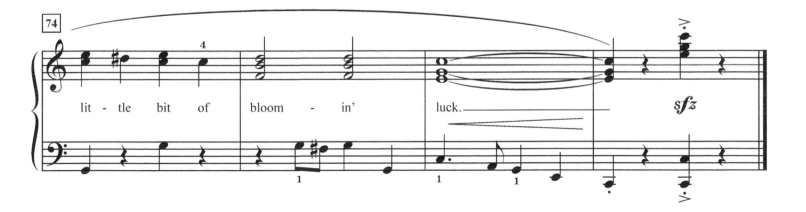

lit - tle bit of bloom - in' luck.
sfz

Just You Wait

Lyrics by Alan Jay Lerner
Music by Frederick Loewe
Arranged by Dan Coates

Passionately

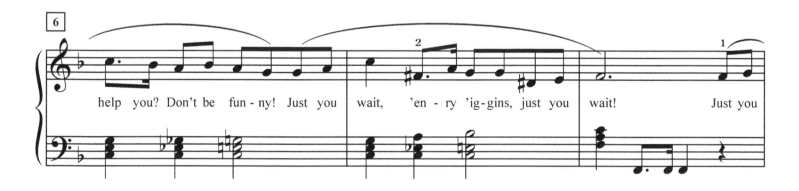

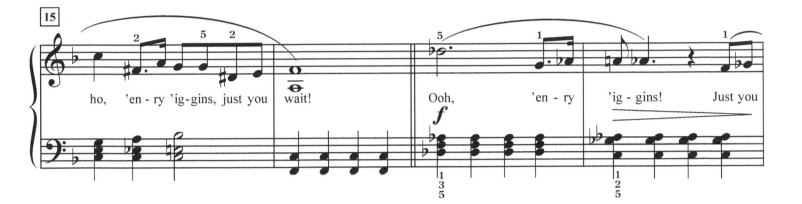

dressed and go to town! Oh, ho, ho, 'en - ry 'ig - gins! Oh, ho, ho, 'en - ry 'ig - gins!

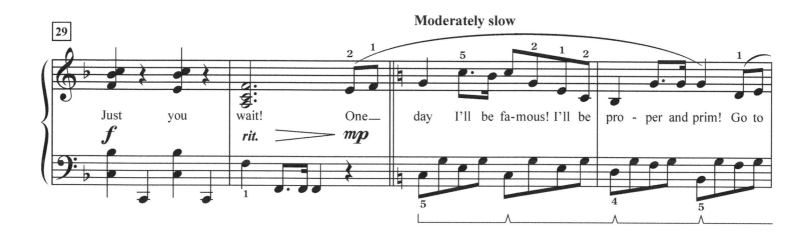

Moderately slow

Just you wait! One— day I'll be fa-mous! I'll be pro - per and prim! Go to

rit. *mp*

Saint James so of - ten I will call it Saint Jim. One— eve - ning the King will say, "Oh,

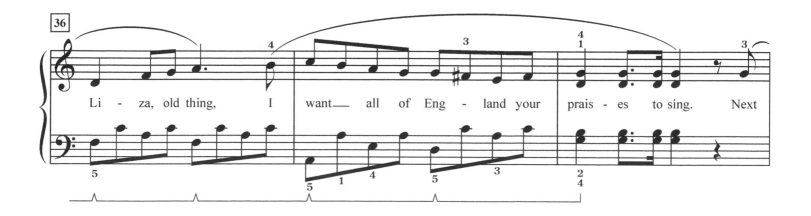

Li - za, old thing, I want— all of Eng - land your prais - es to sing. Next

week, on the twen-ti-eth of May, I pro-claim Li-za Doo-lit-tle Day! All the

a tempo

peo - ple will cel - e - brate the glo - ry of you, and what - ev - er you wish and want I

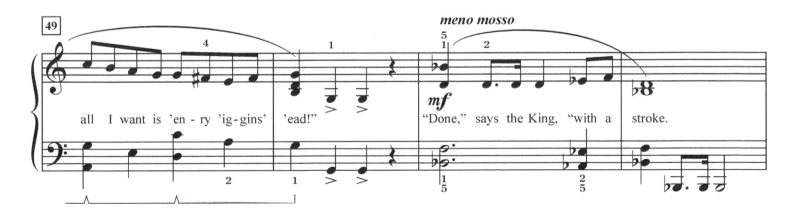

glad - ly will do." "Thanks a lot, King," says I,— in a man - ner well - bred; "But

meno mosso

all I want is 'en - ry 'ig - gins' 'ead!" "Done," says the King, "with a stroke.

Strict march tempo

Guard, run and bring— in the bloke!" Then they'll march you, 'en - ry 'ig - gins, to the

wall; and the King will tell me: "Li - za, sound the call." As they

raise their ri - fles high - er, I'll shout: "Read - y! Aim! Fire!" Oh, ho, ho! 'en - ry 'ig - gins! Down you'll

go! 'en - ry 'ig - gins! Just you wait!

On the Street Where You Live

Lyrics by Alan Jay Lerner
Music by Frederick Loewe
Arranged by Dan Coates

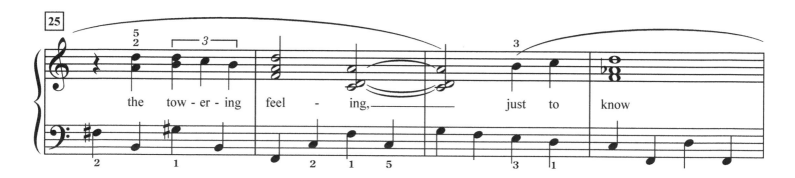

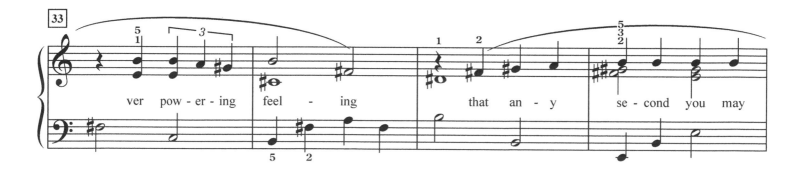

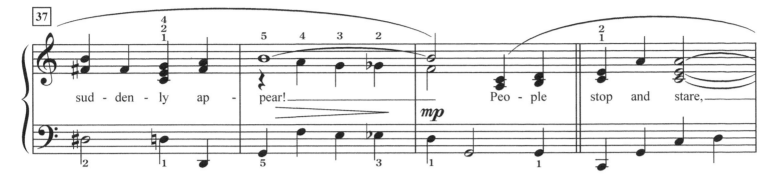

sud - den - ly ap - pear!____ *mp* Peo - ple stop and stare,____

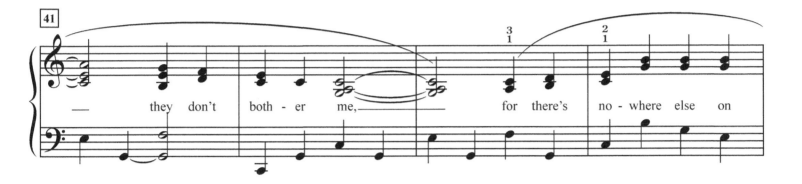

__ they don't both - er me,____ for there's no - where else on

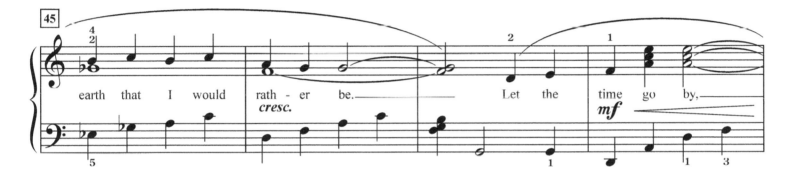

earth that I would rath - er be.____ *cresc.* Let the time go by,____ *mf*

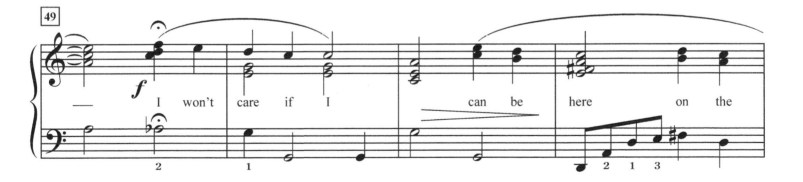

__ *f* I won't care if I can be here on the

street where you live. *rit.* *mp*

The Rain in Spain

Lyrics by Alan Jay Lerner
Music by Frederick Loewe
Arranged by Dan Coates

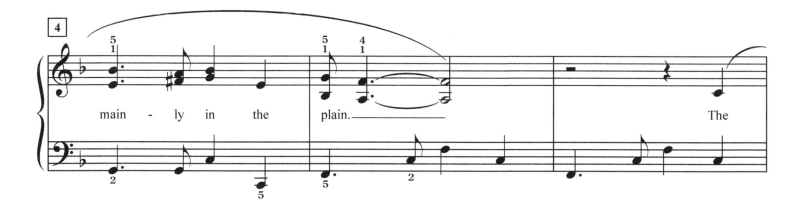

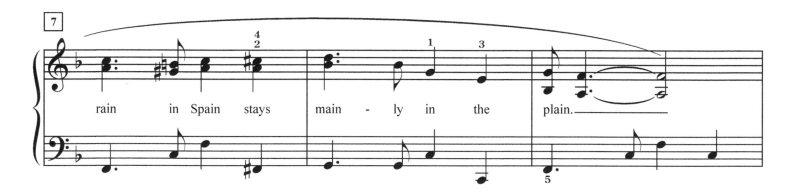

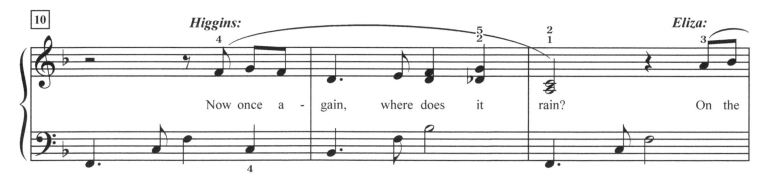

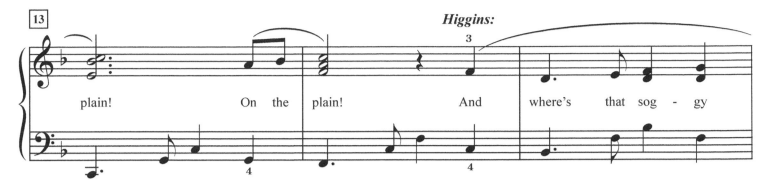

plain!   On   the   plain!   And   where's   that   sog   -   gy

Higgins:

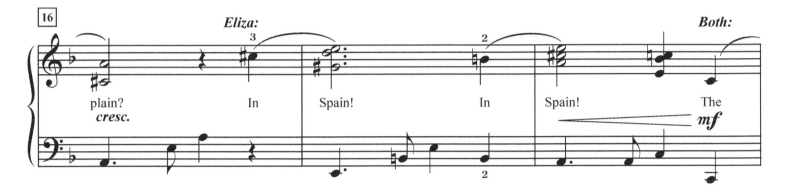

Eliza: *Both:*

plain?   In   Spain!   In   Spain!   The

cresc.   *mf*

rain   in   Spain   stays   main   -   ly   in   the   plain! _____

The   rain   in   Spain   stays   main   -   ly   in   the

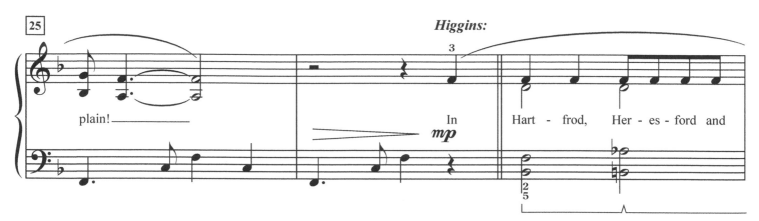

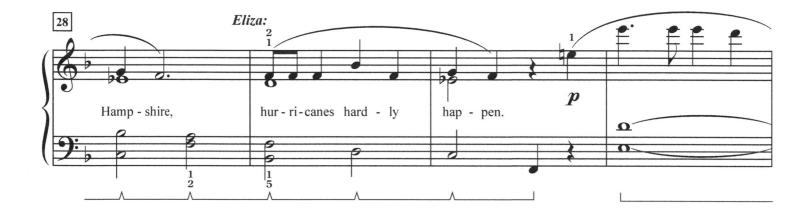

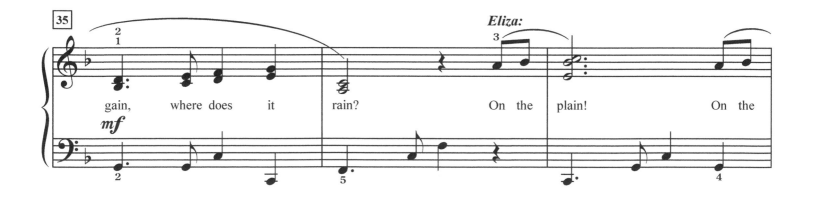

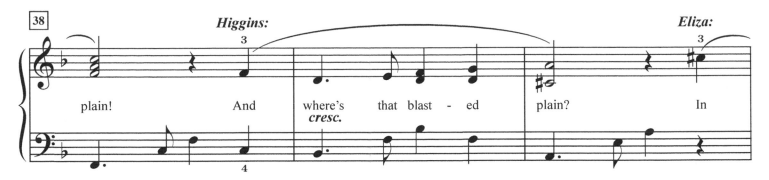

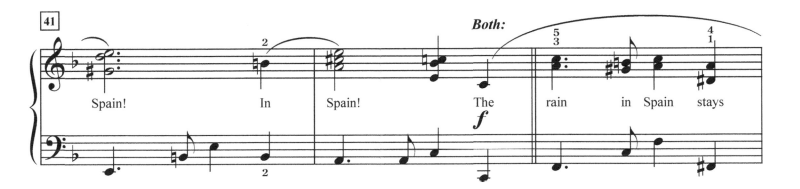

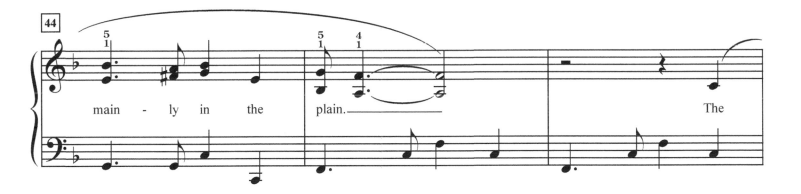

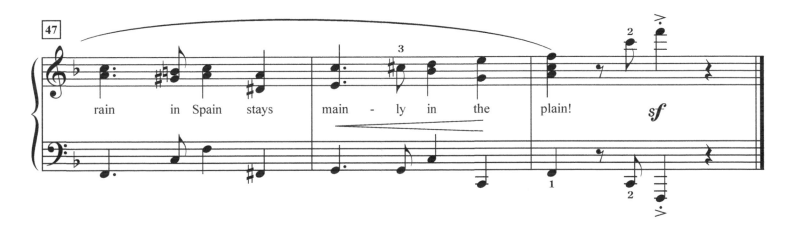

I Could Have Danced All Night

Lyrics by Alan Jay Lerner
Music by Frederick Loewe
Arranged by Dan Coates

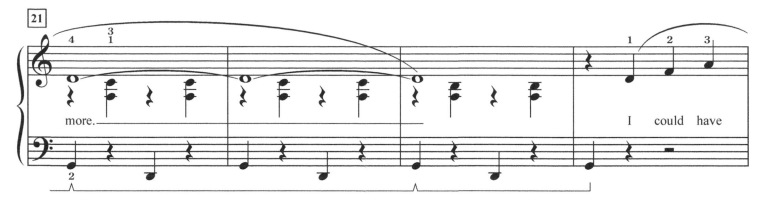

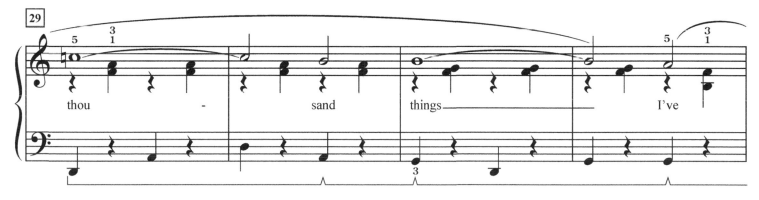

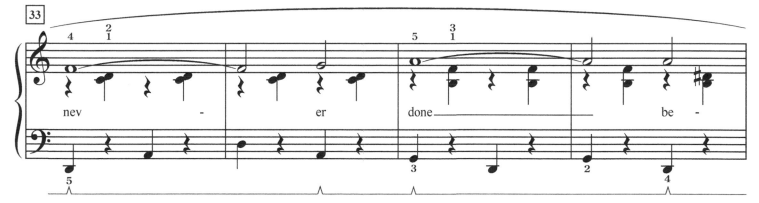

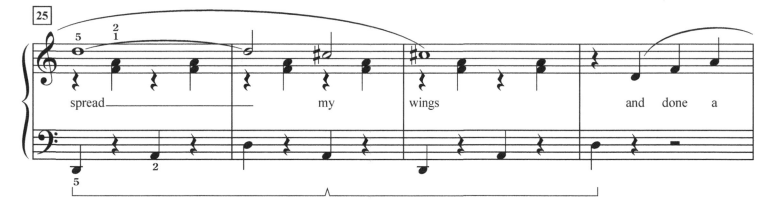

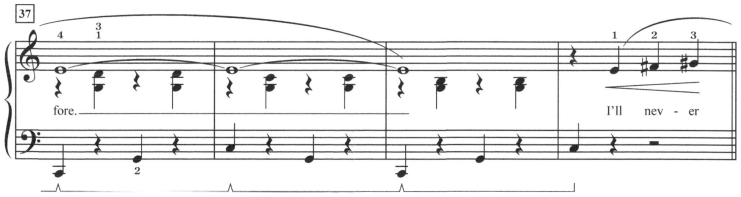

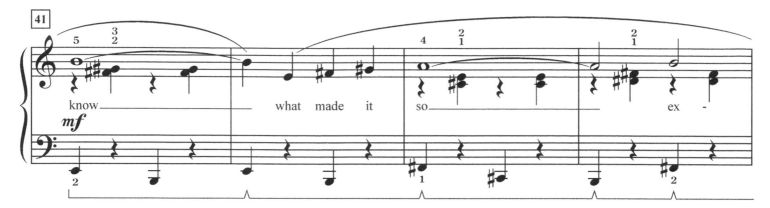

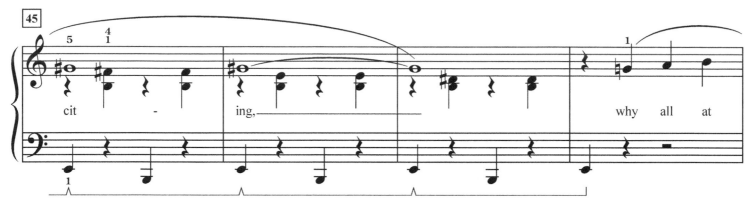

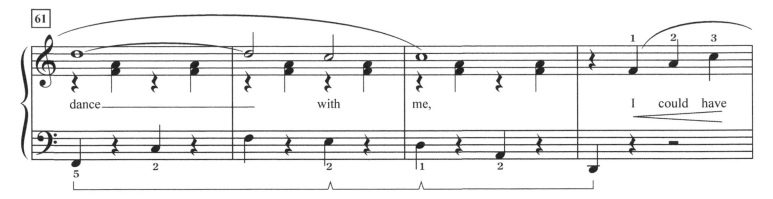

61 dance _____ with me, I could have

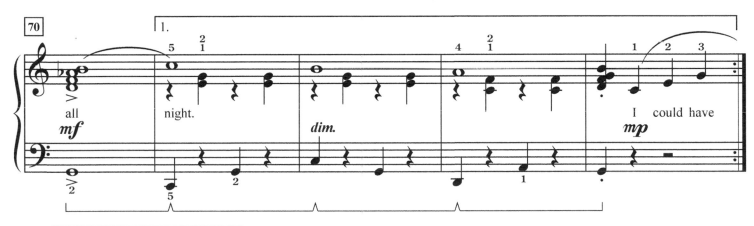

65 danced, *ff* danced, danced _____

70 1. all *mf* night. *dim.* I could have *mp*

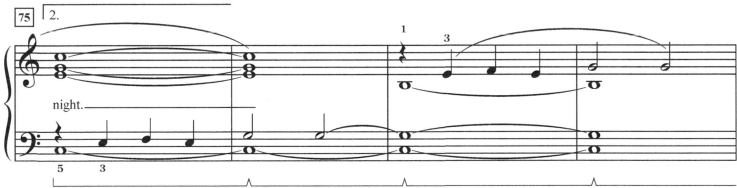

75 2. night. _____

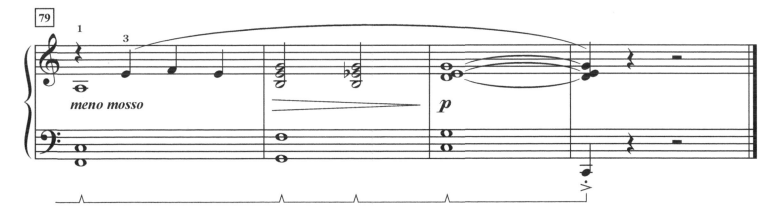

79 *meno mosso* *p*

Show Me

Lyrics by Alan Jay Lerner
Music by Frederick Loewe
Arranged by Dan Coates

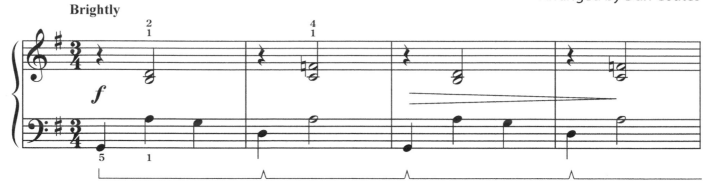

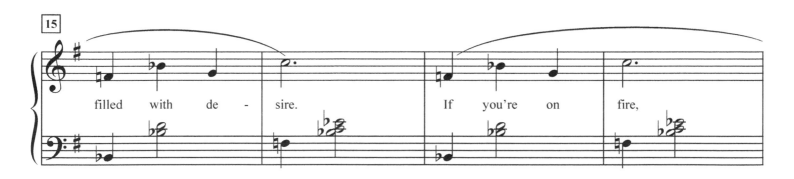

show me! _____

Here we are to-geth-er in the mid-dle of the

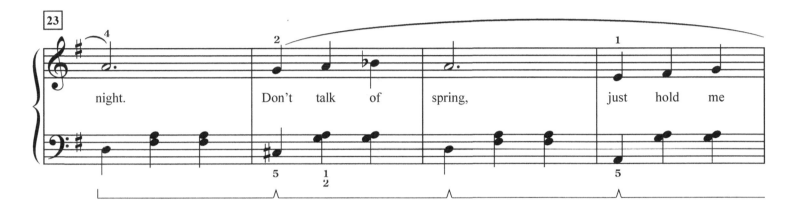

night. Don't talk of spring, just hold me

tight! _____

An-y-one who's ev-er been in love-'ll tell you

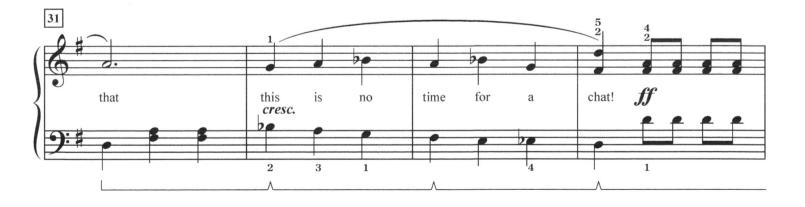

that this is no time for a chat!

cresc.

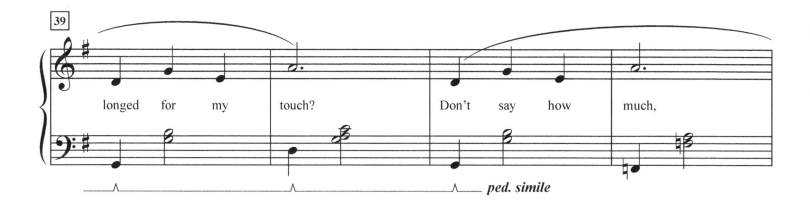

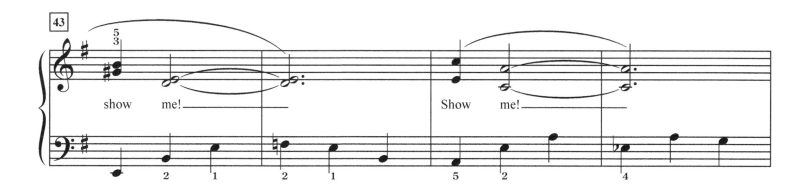

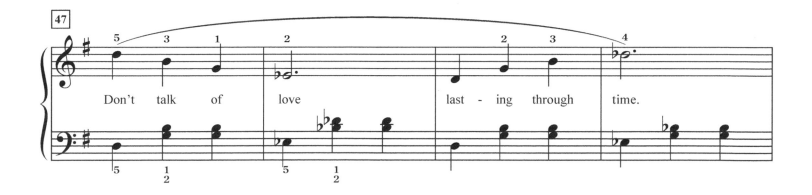

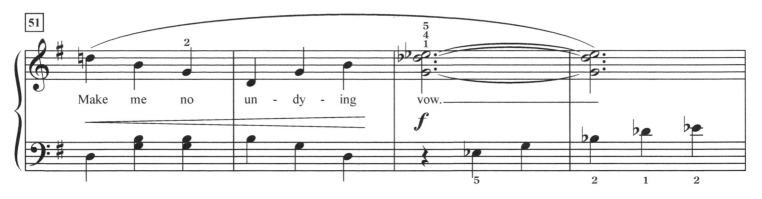

Make me no un - dy - ing vow.

Show me now!

me

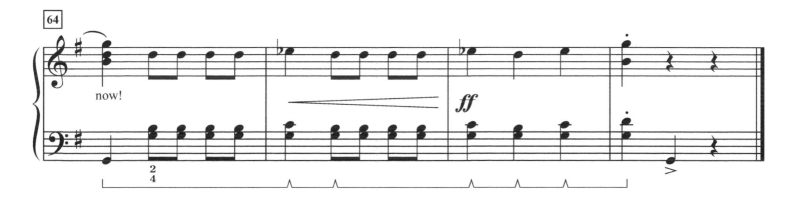

now!

Get Me to the Church on Time

Lyrics by Alan Jay Lerner
Music by Frederick Loewe
Arranged by Dan Coates

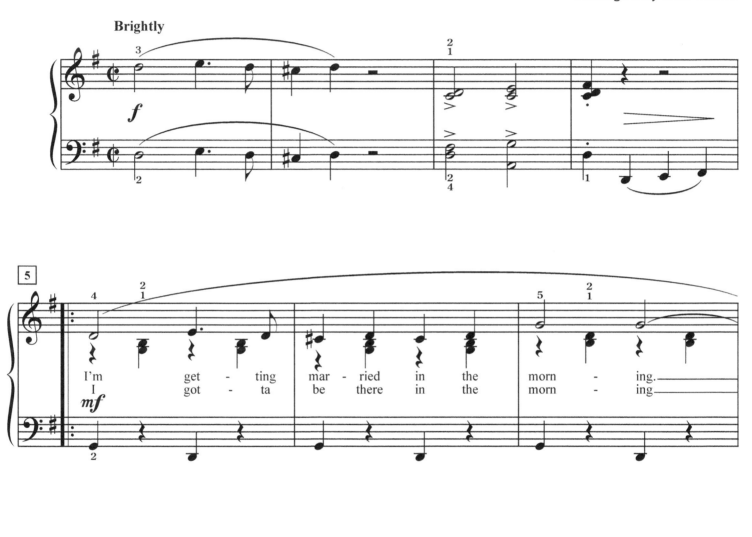

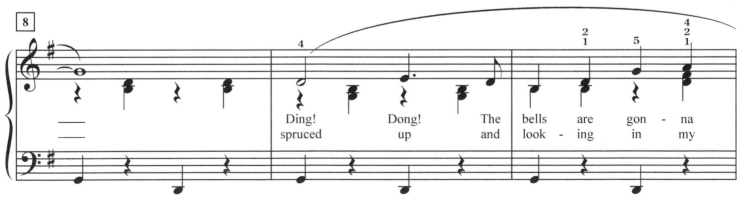

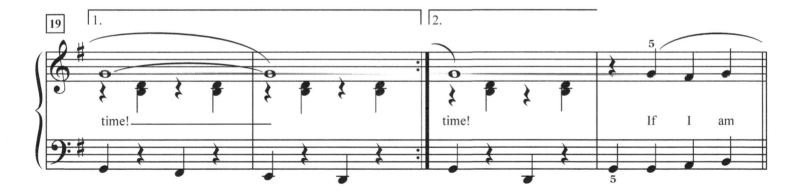

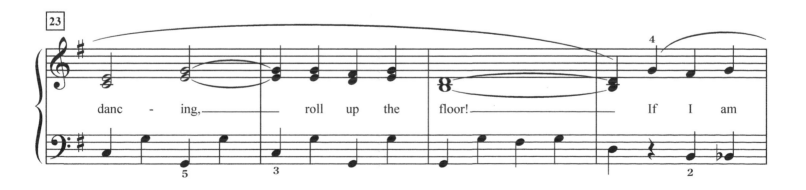

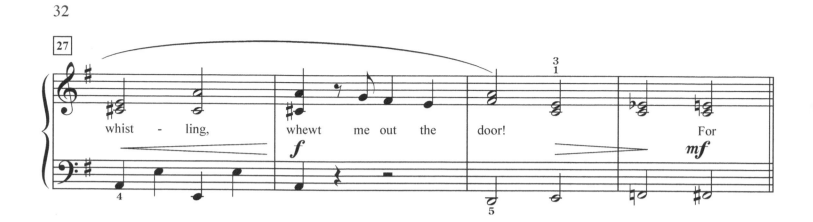

whist - ling,   whewt me out the door!   For

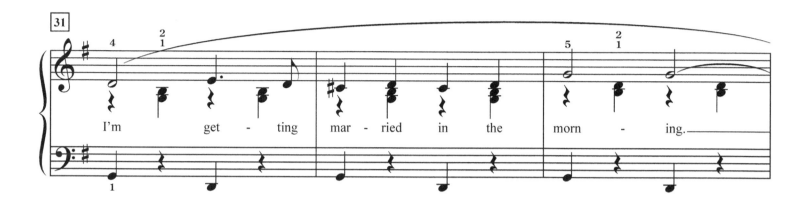

I'm get - ting mar - ried in the morn - ing.

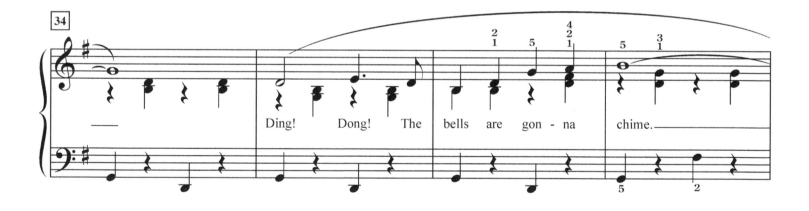

Ding! Dong! The bells are gon - na chime.

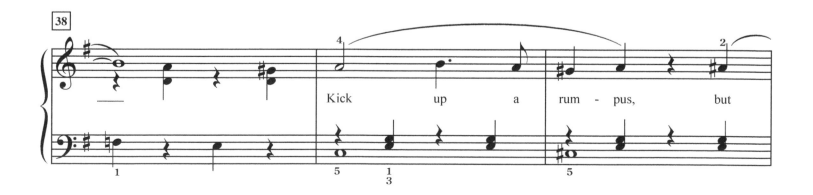

Kick up a rum - pus, but

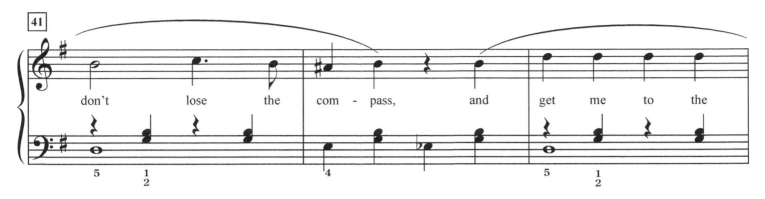

don't   lose   the   com - pass,   and   get   me   to   the

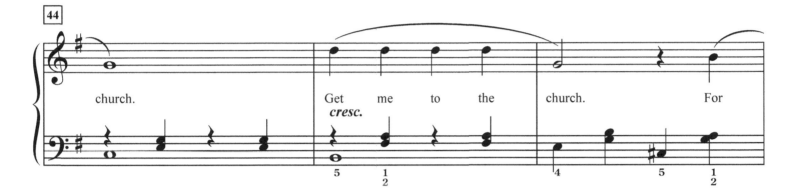

church.   Get   me   to   the   church.   For

cresc.

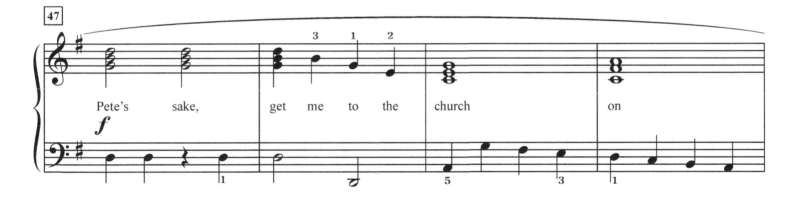

Pete's   sake,   get   me   to   the   church   on

f

time!

sf

Without You

Lyrics by Alan Jay Lerner
Music by Frederick Loewe
Arranged by Dan Coates

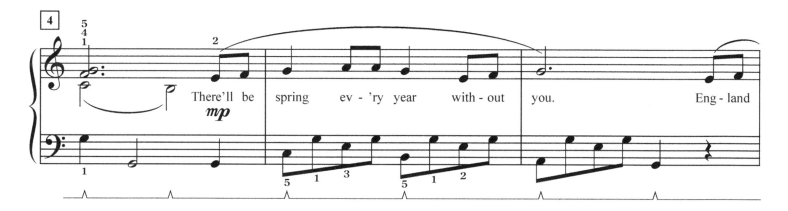

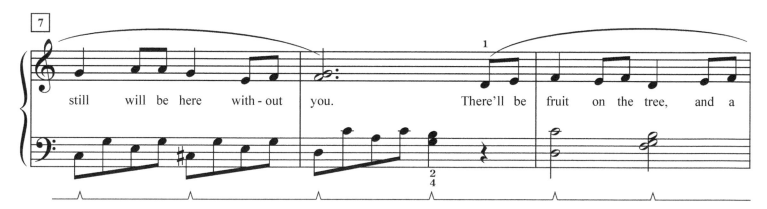

13 mu - sic will thrive with - out you. Some - how Keats will sur - vive with - out

16 you. And there still will be rain on that plain down in Spain, e - ven

19 that will re - main with - out you. I can do

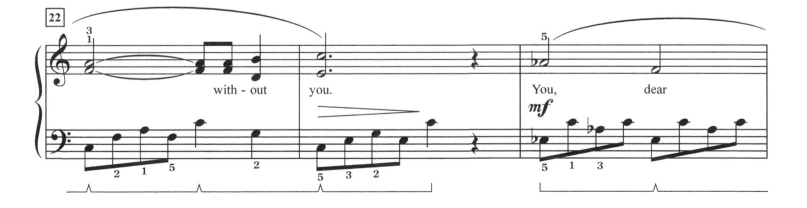

22 with - out you. You, dear

mf

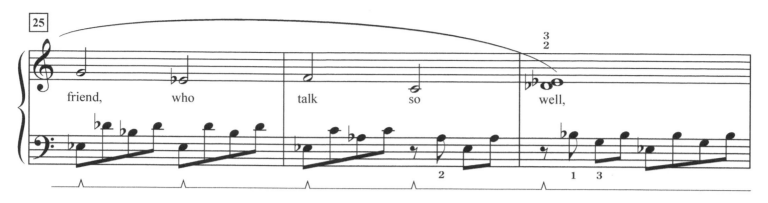

out you pull-ing it, the tide comes in; with-out your twirl-ing it, the earth can spin. With-

out your push-ing them the clouds roll by. If they can do with-out you, duck-y,

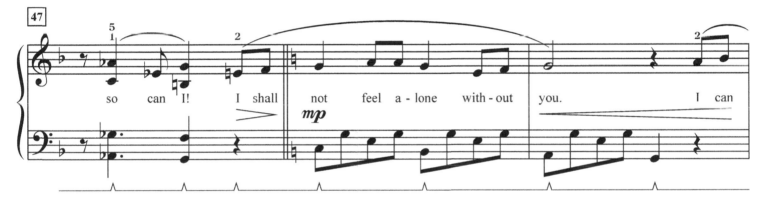

so can I! I shall not feel a-lone with-out you. I can

stand on my own with-out you. So, go back in your shell, I can

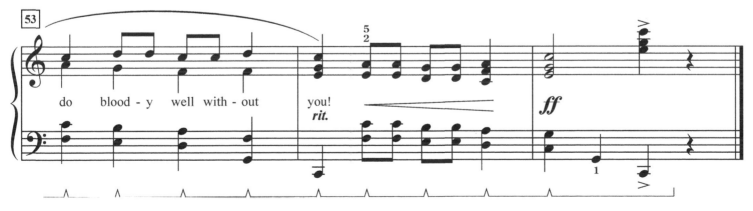

do blood-y well with-out you!

I've Grown Accustomed to Her Face

Lyrics by Alan Jay Lerner
Music by Frederick Loewe
Arranged by Dan Coates

na-ture to me now; like breath-ing out and breath-ing in.
na-ture to me now; like breath-ing out and breath-ing in. I was se -
I'm ver-y

mf

rene - ly in - de - pen-dent and con - tent be-fore we met; sure - ly I could al - ways be that
grate-ful she's a wo - man and so eas - y to for - get; rath - er like a ha - bit one can

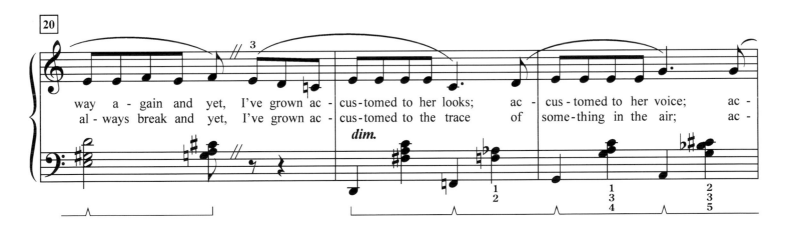

way a - gain and yet, I've grown ac - cus-tomed to her looks; ac - cus-tomed to her voice; ac -
al - ways break and yet, I've grown ac - cus-tomed to the trace of some-thing in the air; ac -

dim.

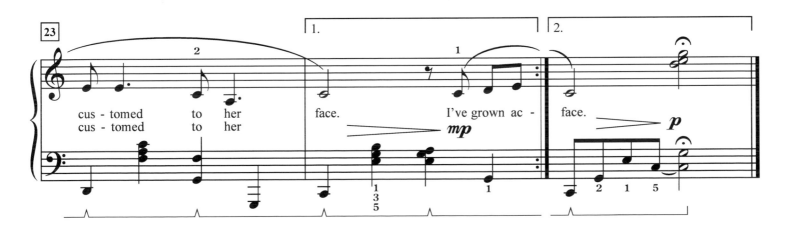

cus - tomed to her face. I've grown ac - face.
cus - tomed to her

mp   *p*